Safeguarding from Blackmail and Online Threats

C. P. Kumar
Reiki Healer
Roorkee - 247667, India

Disclaimer

While every effort has been made to ensure the accuracy and completeness of the content in this book, the author cannot guarantee that the information contained herein is error-free, up-to-date, or suitable for every individual circumstance.

The author shall not be held liable or responsible for any errors or omissions in the content of the book, nor for any damages, or losses that may arise from any actions taken based upon the suggestions or contents presented in the book.

Readers are advised to use their own judgment and discretion in applying the information provided in this book, and to consult with qualified professionals before taking any action based on the contents of this book. The author disclaims any and all liability or responsibility for any actions taken or not taken based on the information contained in this book.

DEDICATION

To all those who refuse to be victims of fear and intimidation, to the brave souls who stand up against the shadows of the digital age, to the champions of privacy, security, and freedom in the online world, this book is dedicated to you.

In a world where technology connects us more than ever before, it has also exposed us to new threats and dangers. But with knowledge comes power, and with power comes resilience.

To the victims of blackmail who found the strength to break free, to the individuals who turned adversity into opportunity, to the experts and advocates tirelessly working to protect us all, your unwavering determination and courage inspire us to delve into the depths of cyber threats, to unravel the intricacies of blackmail, and to shine a light on the path to safety.

This book is dedicated to you, for your strength, your resilience, and your unwavering commitment to safeguarding not only yourselves but also the countless others who seek refuge from the shadows of the digital world.

May your experiences and wisdom serve as a beacon of hope and knowledge, guiding all those who embark on the journey of understanding and defending against online threats.

With utmost respect and gratitude,

C. P. Kumar

CONTENTS

Copyright 2

Disclaimer 3

DEDICATION 4

PREFACE 6

Chapter 1. Understanding Blackmail 9

Chapter 2. Legal Implications........................15

Chapter 3. Recognizing Red Flags 22

Chapter 4. Reporting Blackmail 27

Chapter 5. Personal Safety Measures 32

Chapter 6. Online Privacy.............................37

Chapter 7. Social Media Safety 42

Chapter 8. Email Security.............................46

Chapter 9. Cybersecurity Basics...................52

Chapter 10. Cybersecurity Tools 58

Chapter 11. Password Management................66

Chapter 12. Two-Factor Authentication (2FA)....71

Chapter 13. Protecting Personal Documents......76

Chapter 14. Avoiding Sextortion 83

Chapter 15. Digital Footprint Management 88

Chapter 16. Seeking Help and Support............93

PREFACE

In the ever-evolving landscape of the digital age, we are all explorers, navigating the vast and interconnected web of information, communication, and opportunity. The internet has brought about a world of unprecedented connectivity, empowering us to connect with friends, share our lives, and access a wealth of knowledge at the click of a button. Yet, alongside its countless advantages, this digital realm also harbors unseen dangers, lurking in the shadows, waiting to exploit our vulnerabilities.

The ubiquity of technology has given rise to new forms of threats that transcend the boundaries of physical space. Among these, blackmail and online threats have emerged as formidable adversaries in our digital lives. The consequences of falling victim to these dangers can be both profound and far-reaching, affecting not only our online presence but our peace of mind, personal relationships, and even our legal standing.

This book, "Safeguarding from Blackmail and Online Threats", is your guide to understanding, confronting, and ultimately overcoming these digital adversaries. Within its pages, we embark on a journey to explore the multifaceted world of online threats, beginning with the fundamental question: What is blackmail, and what are its potential consequences?

We delve into the legal implications of blackmail, establishing the seriousness of this offense and the consequences it carries. You'll discover how to recognize red flags, those subtle signs that hint at potential blackmailing attempts, and learn invaluable guidance on what to do if you find yourself ensnared in a web of threats and extortion.

But our journey doesn't end there. This book is your comprehensive resource for enhancing your personal security in daily life, safeguarding your personal information on the internet, and protecting your social media accounts and personal data. We'll explore strategies to prevent phishing and email-based threats, delve into the fundamentals of online security, and equip you with the knowledge to harness the power of cybersecurity tools effectively.

Your passwords will never be the same as we guide you through the intricacies of password management and the added security provided by Two-Factor Authentication (2FA). You'll learn how to keep sensitive documents secure and how to prevent and handle the troubling threats of sextortion.

In an age where our every digital step leaves a trace, we'll explore strategies for managing your digital footprint and minimizing your exposure to potential threats. And for those who find themselves in the darkest corners of cyber danger, we provide a lifeline with resources and guidance on seeking help and support.

The digital world is vast, and the dangers it harbors are real. However, knowledge is our most potent weapon, and through understanding and vigilance, we can protect ourselves and thrive in this new era. This book is your ally, your guardian, and your guide through the labyrinth of online threats. It is our hope that the knowledge you gain here empowers you to navigate the digital world with confidence, resilience, and a steadfast commitment to safeguarding your digital life.

Welcome to "Safeguarding from Blackmail and Online Threats". Together, let us embark on this crucial journey to secure the digital realm and protect what matters most ourselves, our loved ones, and our freedom.

C. P. Kumar

Reiki Healer

Former Scientist 'G', National Institute of Hydrology
Roorkee - 247667, India
Web: https://www.angelfire.com/nh/cpkumar/virgo.html

Introduction

In an era dominated by digital communication and social media, the threat of blackmail has evolved, becoming more insidious and pervasive than ever before. Blackmail is a coercive act that involves the manipulation of sensitive information or secrets to extract money, favors, or compliance from an unwilling victim. This article aims to shed light on the concept of blackmail, its various forms, and the potentially severe consequences it can have on individuals and organizations. By understanding the mechanics and repercussions of blackmail, we can take proactive steps to safeguard ourselves from this ever-present danger.

What is Blackmail?

Blackmail is a malicious and illegal act that typically involves the following components:

Sensitive Information: Blackmailers obtain sensitive, compromising, or embarrassing information about the victim. This information can be in the form of text messages, photos, videos, or any other personal data that, if exposed, would cause harm to the victim's reputation, livelihood, or relationships.

Coercion: Armed with this sensitive information, the blackmailer threatens to disclose it unless the victim complies with their demands. These demands can vary widely, ranging from financial payments to performing certain actions, all of which serve the blackmailer's interests.

Intent: The primary intent behind blackmail is personal gain. Blackmailers aim to benefit from their victim's fear and desperation, whether it be financial gain, revenge, or exerting control over the victim.

Forms of Blackmail

Blackmail comes in various forms, often adapting to the technological advancements of the time. Some common forms of blackmail include:

Traditional Blackmail: This involves handwritten letters, photographs, or other physical evidence. The blackmailer sends these materials to the victim or relevant parties, threatening to release the compromising information unless their demands are met.

Digital Blackmail: With the rise of technology, digital blackmail has become increasingly prevalent. This form involves the use of electronic media such as emails, social media messages, or encrypted messaging apps to communicate threats. The blackmailer may possess explicit photos or messages and threatens to share them unless the victim complies.

Revenge Porn: A particularly heinous form of digital blackmail, revenge porn involves the distribution of explicit photos or videos of a victim without their consent. Perpetrators may demand money or further explicit content from the victim in exchange for not sharing the materials with a broader audience.

Financial Blackmail: In this form, the blackmailer threatens to reveal financial improprieties or secrets, which could lead to severe legal or professional consequences for the victim. The victim is coerced into paying a substantial sum of money to prevent exposure.

The Consequences of Blackmail

Blackmail can have far-reaching and devastating consequences for both individuals and organizations. Here are some of the potential outcomes:

Emotional Distress: Victims of blackmail often experience extreme emotional distress, including anxiety, depression, and even thoughts of self-harm. The constant fear of exposure takes a severe toll on mental well-being.

Damage to Reputation: If the sensitive information is released, it can cause significant harm to the victim's reputation. This can result in the loss of personal relationships, damage to professional prospects, and social isolation.

Financial Loss: Victims may be coerced into paying significant sums of money to their blackmailer. This financial loss can be crippling, leading to debt, bankruptcy, or the depletion of savings.

Legal Consequences: Blackmail is a crime in many jurisdictions. If the blackmailer is caught and prosecuted, they could face imprisonment and fines. However, victims may also face legal repercussions if the sensitive information involves criminal activities.

Impact on Relationships: The exposure of sensitive information can damage personal relationships irreparably. Friends, family members, and colleagues may distance themselves from the victim, believing the information to be true.

Loss of Control: Victims of blackmail often feel helpless and manipulated, as they are forced to comply with the blackmailer's demands against their will. This loss of control over their own lives can be traumatic.

Continued Exploitation: Paying a blackmailer does not guarantee that they will cease their activities. In fact, victims who comply with demands may become targets for future blackmail attempts.

How to Safeguard Against Blackmail

Protecting oneself from blackmail requires a proactive approach. Here are some strategies to safeguard against blackmail:

Be Cautious Online: Be mindful of the information you share online, especially on social media. Avoid sharing sensitive information or engaging in risky behaviors that could be used against you.

Maintain Strong Passwords: Use complex, unique passwords for your online accounts. Enable two-factor authentication wherever possible to add an extra layer of security.

Educate Yourself: Familiarize yourself with the common tactics used by blackmailers, such as phishing emails and social engineering. Phishing emails are fraudulent messages designed to deceive recipients into revealing sensitive information or taking harmful actions. Social engineering is the manipulation of individuals to divulge confidential information or perform actions that compromise security. Be cautious when interacting with unfamiliar individuals online.

Secure Your Devices: **Regularly update your devices and use reputable antivirus software to protect against malware and hacking attempts.**

Document Threats: **If you receive threats, document them carefully. Save messages, emails, or any other communication from the blackmailer. This evidence can be crucial if you decide to involve law enforcement.**

Seek Support: **Reach out to friends, family members, or professionals if you believe you are a victim of blackmail. Do not suffer in silence; support can make a significant difference.**

Report to Authorities: **If you believe you are a victim of blackmail, report it to the relevant authorities immediately. Law enforcement agencies have experience dealing with such cases and can help you navigate the situation.**

Consider Legal Action: **Consult with an attorney to explore the possibility of legal action against the blackmailer. Laws regarding blackmail vary by jurisdiction, so it's essential to understand your rights and options.**

Conclusion

Blackmail is a menacing threat that can have severe and long-lasting consequences for individuals and organizations. In today's digital age, it has become easier for blackmailers to exploit their victims through various means. Understanding what blackmail is, its different forms, and the potential consequences is the first step in safeguarding oneself against this threat.

By staying vigilant, practicing online security measures, and seeking help when needed, individuals can reduce their vulnerability to blackmail. Remember that blackmail is a crime, and there are legal avenues available to combat it. With the right knowledge and resources, we can all work towards a safer and more secure digital environment, free from the shadow of blackmail and its devastating effects.

Introduction

Blackmail is a grave offense that strikes at the heart of personal privacy and security. It involves the coercive threat of revealing sensitive, embarrassing, or damaging information about an individual unless they comply with the blackmailer's demands. While blackmail is commonly portrayed in popular culture, its legal implications are often misunderstood or underestimated. In this article, we will delve into the legal aspects of blackmail, exploring its definition, elements, consequences, and the importance of safeguarding oneself from such threats. Understanding the seriousness of blackmail is crucial for individuals, businesses, and society as a whole.

Defining Blackmail

Blackmail is a criminal act that involves the use of threats to force someone into taking a specific action against their will. At its core, blackmail includes three essential elements:

Threat: To constitute blackmail, there must be a clear and explicit threat made by the blackmailer. This threat can take various forms, such as exposing embarrassing information, revealing a secret, or causing harm to the victim's reputation, career, or personal life.

Demand: A demand is made by the blackmailer, specifying what action they want the victim to take to prevent the threatened harm. Common demands include the payment of money, providing confidential information, or performing illegal activities on the blackmailer's behalf.

Consideration: The victim must comply with the blackmailer's demand in response to the threat. This compliance is typically the result of fear, coercion, or the belief that the blackmailer has the means to carry out the threat.

Legal Implications of Blackmail

Blackmail is a criminal offense in most jurisdictions, and the legal implications can vary from one place to another. However, common legal consequences of blackmail include:

Criminal Charges: Blackmail is a criminal offense that can lead to charges against the perpetrator. Depending on the jurisdiction and the severity of the offense, these charges may include extortion, harassment, or coercion. Convictions can result in substantial fines and imprisonment.

Civil Lawsuits: Victims of blackmail can also pursue civil lawsuits against the blackmailer. These lawsuits may seek damages for emotional distress, loss of reputation, or financial harm caused by the blackmail.

Damaging Reputation: Being accused or convicted of blackmail can have long-lasting negative effects on a person's reputation and social standing. It can damage personal and professional relationships and result in social isolation.

Legal Record: A conviction for blackmail can create a criminal record, which can affect a person's ability to secure employment, housing, or certain licenses and certifications.

Restitution: Courts may order the blackmailer to compensate the victim for any financial losses incurred as a result of the blackmail. This can include repaying any money extorted or covering the cost of therapy or counseling for emotional distress.

Consequences for Perpetrators

Blackmailers who are caught and convicted can face severe legal consequences. These consequences are intended to serve as a deterrent to others and to uphold the principles of justice. The specific penalties for blackmail can vary widely depending on the jurisdiction, the severity of the offense, and the presence of aggravating factors. Here are some potential legal consequences for blackmailers:

Imprisonment: In many jurisdictions, blackmail is a felony offense that can lead to a significant period of imprisonment. The length of the sentence may depend on factors such as the seriousness of the threats, the extent of the harm caused, and the presence of prior criminal convictions.

Fines: Convicted blackmailers may be required to pay substantial fines as part of their sentence. These fines are meant to provide restitution to the victim and to deter future criminal behavior.

Probation: Some individuals convicted of blackmail may be placed on probation, which involves strict supervision and adherence to certain conditions, such as regular check-ins with a probation officer and compliance with a restraining order to protect the victim.

Restitution: Courts may order the blackmailer to pay restitution to the victim, covering any financial losses they incurred as a result of the blackmail. This can include repaying extorted money or compensating for other damages.

Criminal Record: A conviction for blackmail can result in a permanent criminal record, which can have far-reaching consequences for the individual's future employment prospects, housing opportunities, and social relationships.

Civil Lawsuits: In addition to criminal penalties, blackmailers may also face civil lawsuits filed by their victims. These lawsuits can result in the payment of significant monetary damages.

The Importance of Safeguarding Against Blackmail

Preventing blackmail is essential not only for individuals but also for businesses, government agencies, and organizations of all sizes. Here are some key reasons why safeguarding against blackmail is of utmost importance:

Protecting Personal Privacy: Blackmail can invade an individual's privacy by exposing personal, sensitive, or embarrassing information. Safeguarding against blackmail helps protect personal privacy and prevent the unauthorized disclosure of such information.

Preventing Financial Losses: Many blackmailers demand money or valuable assets from their victims. By safeguarding against blackmail, individuals and organizations can avoid financial losses and the potential economic harm associated with compliance.

Upholding Ethical Standards: Blackmail often involves illegal and unethical activities. By taking steps to prevent blackmail, individuals and organizations can uphold their ethical standards and avoid involvement in criminal behavior.

Maintaining Reputation: Blackmail can tarnish an individual's or organization's reputation. Preventing blackmail helps protect reputation and credibility in the eyes of peers, customers, and the public.

Ensuring Legal Compliance: Engaging in blackmail can lead to criminal charges and legal consequences. By safeguarding against blackmail, individuals and organizations ensure that they remain on the right side of the law.

Safeguarding Against Blackmail

Preventing blackmail involves proactive steps to minimize the risk of becoming a victim. Here are some strategies and best practices for safeguarding against blackmail:

Protect Personal Information: Individuals should be cautious about sharing personal information online and offline. Use strong, unique passwords for online accounts and avoid sharing sensitive information with unknown or unverified individuals.

Be Wary of Unsolicited Requests: Be cautious when receiving unsolicited messages, especially those that ask for personal information or make unusual demands. Verify the identity of the sender before taking any action.

Educate Yourself: Familiarize yourself with the legal definition of blackmail and its consequences in your jurisdiction. Knowing your rights and understanding the legal framework can help you respond appropriately if you become a victim.

Document Threats: If you receive blackmail threats, document them carefully. Save messages, emails, or any evidence of the threats, as this documentation can be crucial in legal proceedings.

Report Threats: If you receive blackmail threats, report them to law enforcement authorities. They can investigate the matter and take appropriate action against the perpetrator.

Seek Legal Advice: If you believe you are a victim of blackmail or if you have concerns about potential threats, consult with an attorney who specializes in criminal law. They can provide guidance on how to protect your rights and interests.

Maintain Strong Security Practices: Use up-to-date antivirus software, firewalls, and other security measures to protect your digital devices and data from potential hackers and blackmailers.

Be Cautious on Social Media: Be mindful of the information you share on social media platforms. Avoid disclosing sensitive personal details that could be used against you.

Conclusion

Blackmail is a serious offense with significant legal and personal consequences for both perpetrators and victims. Understanding the legal aspects of blackmail and its consequences is essential for individuals and organizations alike. By taking proactive steps to safeguard against blackmail, individuals can protect their personal privacy, financial well-being, and reputation, while also upholding ethical standards and legal compliance. Reporting threats and seeking legal advice when necessary are critical steps in addressing blackmail and holding perpetrators accountable for their actions. In a world where personal information is increasingly vulnerable, safeguarding against blackmail is an important aspect of personal security and societal well-being.

Introduction

In our increasingly digital world, the threat of blackmail and online threats looms larger than ever before. Blackmailers exploit personal information and leverage it against their victims to extort money, favors, or other forms of compliance. To effectively safeguard ourselves from these malicious actors, it's crucial to recognize the red flags that often precede blackmailing attempts. In this article, we will explore the various warning signs and techniques to identify potential blackmailing attempts, empowering you to protect your privacy and security online.

Unusual Requests for Personal Information

One of the initial red flags to watch out for is receiving unsolicited requests for personal information. Be wary of individuals or organizations that ask for sensitive data such as your social security number, bank account details, or intimate photos. These requests may be disguised as seemingly innocent inquiries or offers, but their intent is often malicious. Legitimate entities rarely require such sensitive information without proper verification.

Aggressive or Threatening Communication

Blackmailers often resort to aggressive or threatening communication tactics to intimidate their victims. If you receive messages, emails, or phone calls filled with threats, derogatory language, or ominous warnings, it's a clear indication that someone is attempting to manipulate you through fear. These tactics are designed to make you more susceptible to their demands.

Unusual Friend Requests or Followers on Social Media

Social media platforms can be fertile ground for blackmailers looking to gather personal information or compromising content. Be cautious of unsolicited friend requests or followers, especially from profiles with limited information and a suspicious number of friends or followers. These individuals may be trying to gain access to your personal life, gather information, or establish a connection for future extortion.

Unsolicited Messages or Emails with Personal Content

Pay close attention to unsolicited messages or emails that contain personal information about you or your loved ones. Blackmailers may attempt to build rapport by sharing information they claim to know about you, your family, or your activities. They use this information to create a sense of vulnerability and make their threats appear more credible.

Coercive Sharing of Intimate Content

One of the most common forms of blackmail involves the coercive sharing of intimate or compromising content. If someone threatens to expose private photos, videos, or messages, it's a clear indication of blackmail. These individuals may use the threat of public humiliation as leverage to extort money or other favors. Always exercise caution when sharing sensitive material and be mindful of whom you trust.

Requests for Money or Valuables

Blackmailers often have financial motives, and they may directly request money or valuable items in exchange for not revealing compromising information. These demands can be made through various channels, including text messages, emails, or even physical letters. Any request for money or valuables from an unknown or suspicious source should raise immediate suspicion.

Manipulative Emotional Appeals

Some blackmailers use manipulative emotional appeals to gain their victims' sympathy and compliance. They may claim to be in dire straits, facing personal crises, or even threaten self-harm if their demands are not met. While these appeals can be emotionally distressing, it's important to remain skeptical and consider the possibility of manipulation.

Rapid Escalation of Threats

Blackmailers often escalate their threats over time to increase the pressure on their victims. Initially, they may make subtle hints or veiled threats, but as resistance persists, their tactics become more aggressive. Recognizing this pattern can help you take action before the situation becomes more dangerous.

Inconsistent or Unverifiable Claims

Blackmailers may make claims about having damaging information, but they often provide inconsistent or unverifiable details. They might lack concrete evidence to support their threats. Requesting proof or verification can help you assess the legitimacy of their claims.

Involvement of Unusual Online Platforms

Be cautious if a blackmailer directs you to communicate through obscure or untraceable online platforms. These may include messaging apps with end-to-end encryption, anonymous email services, or cryptocurrency transactions. Such platforms make it challenging to track and report malicious activities, providing a level of anonymity to the extortionist.

Multiple Victims or Recipients

If you discover that you are not the only recipient of threatening messages or blackmail attempts from the same source, it's a strong indicator of a coordinated extortion effort. Sharing your experiences and collaborating with other victims can be essential in gathering evidence and reporting the situation to the authorities.

Seeking Professional Advice and Assistance

When you encounter red flags that suggest a potential blackmailing attempt, it's crucial to seek professional advice and assistance. Law enforcement agencies, cybercrime units, and legal experts specialize in dealing with such cases. Do not hesitate to report the incident and provide any evidence you may have.

Conclusion

Recognizing red flags is the first step in protecting yourself from potential blackmailing attempts and online threats. By staying vigilant and learning to identify the warning signs discussed in this article, you can reduce your vulnerability and respond effectively if you become a target. Remember that seeking help from law enforcement and legal experts is crucial in dealing with blackmail situations, as they have the knowledge and resources to investigate and address these crimes. In an age where digital privacy is paramount, arming yourself with the knowledge to recognize and respond to blackmail attempts is a vital aspect of safeguarding your online security.

Introduction

Blackmail is a harrowing and illegal act that can have severe consequences for the victim. It involves the threat of revealing embarrassing, disgraceful, or damaging information about a person unless they comply with the blackmailer's demands. In today's digital age, online blackmail has become increasingly prevalent, making it crucial for individuals to know how to respond effectively if they find themselves in such a distressing situation. This article offers comprehensive guidance on how to handle blackmail and the importance of reporting it.

Understanding Blackmail

1. Defining Blackmail

Blackmail is a criminal offense in which one party threatens to expose sensitive or damaging information about another unless they fulfill specific demands. This information could be personal, financial, or any other data that the victim wishes to keep confidential.

2. Recognizing the Elements of Blackmail

To identify blackmail, one must understand its elements:

Threat: The blackmailer makes a clear and explicit threat to disclose the information.

Demand: The blackmailer specifies what they want from the victim in exchange for not revealing the information.

Confidential Information: The blackmailer possesses sensitive information that the victim wants to keep secret.

Responding to Blackmail

1. Stay Calm and Do Not Give in to Fear

When faced with blackmail, it is natural to feel frightened, embarrassed, or anxious. However, it is essential to remain calm and avoid making hasty decisions. Panic can cloud judgment and lead to poor choices.

2. Do Not Comply with the Blackmailer's Demands

Giving in to a blackmailer's demands may provide temporary relief but will likely lead to further exploitation. It reinforces the blackmailer's behavior and encourages them to continue their criminal activities.

3. Preserve Evidence

It is crucial to gather and preserve all evidence related to the blackmail. This includes messages, emails, or any other communication that documents the threats and demands. This evidence will be valuable when reporting the incident to the authorities.

4. Block and Restrict Contact

If the blackmailer is reaching out through digital channels, block their contact and restrict their access to your personal information. This can help prevent further harassment.

Reporting Blackmail

1. Contact Law Enforcement

Reporting blackmail to law enforcement is a critical step in addressing the issue. Reach out to your local police department or cybercrime unit and provide them with all the evidence you have collected. They can guide you through the process of filing a formal report.

2. Seek Legal Counsel

Consult with an attorney who specializes in cybercrimes or blackmail cases. They can offer legal advice and support, helping you understand your rights and options.

3. Inform Trusted Individuals

Share the situation with people you trust, such as friends and family. They can provide emotional support and may be witnesses or character references if needed during legal proceedings.

4. Utilize Victim Support Services

Victim support services and organizations can provide valuable assistance during and after a blackmail incident. They offer emotional support, resources, and guidance to help victims navigate the challenges they face.

Protecting Your Online Presence

1. Strengthen Online Security

To prevent future blackmail attempts, enhance your online security measures. This includes using strong and unique passwords, enabling two-factor authentication, and being cautious about sharing personal information online.

2. Regularly Monitor Your Online Presence

Be proactive in monitoring your online presence and personal information. Regularly review your social media profiles, online accounts, and privacy settings to ensure they are secure.

3. Educate Yourself About Cybersecurity

Understanding cybersecurity best practices can help you avoid falling victim to blackmail and other online threats. Stay informed about the latest online risks and how to protect yourself.

Legal Recourse

1. Civil Lawsuits

In addition to criminal charges, victims of blackmail may also pursue civil lawsuits against the blackmailer to seek damages for emotional distress, financial losses, and reputational harm.

2. Cyberbullying and Harassment Laws

Familiarize yourself with the laws and regulations in your jurisdiction related to cyberbullying, harassment, and online threats. These laws may vary from one location to another.

Conclusion

Blackmail is a distressing and unlawful act that can have severe consequences for both victims and perpetrators. It is essential to respond to blackmail calmly, without giving in to fear or compliance. Reporting the blackmail to law enforcement and seeking legal advice are crucial steps in addressing the issue. Furthermore, safeguarding your online presence, educating yourself about cybersecurity, and understanding your legal options can help protect you from future threats.

Remember that you are not alone in facing blackmail; there are support services and professionals available to guide you through the process of reporting and recovering from this traumatic experience. By taking these steps and standing up against blackmail, you can assert your rights, protect your well-being, and contribute to a safer online environment for all.

Introduction

In today's digital age, personal safety has taken on a new dimension. With the advent of technology and the increasing prevalence of online threats, safeguarding oneself from blackmail and other dangers has become more crucial than ever. This article will delve into the various steps individuals can take to enhance their personal security in daily life, both online and offline. By following these measures, you can minimize the risk of falling victim to blackmail and online threats.

Strengthening Physical Security

1. Home Security

Ensuring the safety of your home is the first step in enhancing your personal security. This involves installing robust locks, security systems, and surveillance cameras. Additionally, consider reinforcing windows and doors to make it more difficult for potential intruders to gain access.

2. Personal Alarms

Carry personal alarms or panic buttons when venturing into unfamiliar or potentially dangerous areas. These devices emit loud noises when activated, alerting others to your distress and potentially deterring attackers.

3. Self-Defense Training

Taking self-defense classes can empower you with the skills and confidence needed to protect yourself in physically threatening situations. Knowledge of basic self-defense techniques can prove invaluable.

Online Security

1. Strong Passwords

Create strong, unique passwords for each of your online accounts. Use a combination of letters, numbers, and special characters, and avoid using easily guessable information like birthdays or names. Consider using a reputable password manager to keep track of your passwords securely.

2. Two-Factor Authentication (2FA)

Enable two-factor authentication whenever possible. This adds an extra layer of security by requiring you to enter a temporary code sent to your mobile device or email after entering your password.

3. Regular Software Updates

Keep your devices and software up to date. Updates often include security patches that protect against known vulnerabilities. Neglecting updates can leave you vulnerable to online threats.

4. Safe Browsing Habits

Exercise caution when clicking on links or downloading files, especially from unknown sources. Be wary of phishing attempts, and always verify the authenticity of websites before entering personal information.

5. Privacy Settings

Review and adjust the privacy settings on your social media profiles and other online accounts. Limit the amount of personal information you share publicly, as this information can be used by malicious actors for blackmail or identity theft.

Protecting Personal Information

1. Shredding Documents

Dispose of sensitive documents by shredding them rather than throwing them in the trash. In the context of online activities, shredding documents typically refers to securely deleting or permanently erasing digital files or data to protect sensitive information and maintain online privacy and security. Identity thieves can exploit discarded documents containing personal information.

2. Secure Personal Devices

Set up PINs, passwords, or biometric locks on your smartphones, tablets, and laptops to prevent unauthorized access to your personal information in case of theft or loss.

3. Guard Personal Information

Be cautious about sharing personal information, both online and offline. Only provide sensitive information to trusted entities and avoid disclosing unnecessary details.

Online Communication Safety

1. Email Encryption

Consider using encrypted email services for sensitive communications. Encryption ensures that only the intended recipient can access the content of your emails.

2. Secure Messaging Apps

Use secure messaging apps that offer end-to-end encryption for sensitive conversations. These apps provide an extra layer of protection against eavesdropping. Eavesdropping is the act of secretly listening to or monitoring private conversations, often without the knowledge or consent of the parties involved, and it can occur in various contexts, including in-person or electronically over communication channels.

3. Social Media Caution

Be mindful of what you share on social media platforms. Oversharing personal information or posting compromising content can make you vulnerable to blackmail.

Trust Your Instincts

Trust your instincts. If something doesn't feel right, whether it's an online interaction or a real-life situation, take it seriously. It's better to be cautious than to ignore potential dangers.

Seek Professional Help

If you suspect you are a victim of online threats or blackmail, don't hesitate to seek the assistance of cybersecurity experts or law enforcement. They can help you identify and mitigate the threats effectively.

Conclusion

Enhancing personal security in daily life is a multifaceted endeavor that encompasses both physical and digital aspects. By strengthening home security, adopting safe online practices, protecting personal information, and trusting your instincts, you can reduce the risk of falling victim to blackmail and online threats. Remember that your safety is paramount, and taking proactive steps to safeguard yourself is an investment in your well-being and peace of mind in an increasingly interconnected world. Stay vigilant, stay secure.

Introduction

In our increasingly digital world, where personal information is shared, stored, and transmitted online, safeguarding our privacy has never been more critical. With the rise of cyber threats, identity theft, and data breaches, it's essential to take proactive steps to protect our personal information on the internet. This article will provide valuable tips on how to enhance your online privacy and reduce the risk of falling victim to blackmail and other online threats.

Strong Passwords and Authentication

One of the first lines of defense in protecting your online privacy is to establish strong, unique passwords for all your accounts. Avoid using easily guessable information like birthdays or common words. Instead, create complex passwords that combine upper and lower case letters, numbers, and special characters. Additionally, it's crucial to use a different password for each online account to minimize the potential damage if one gets compromised.

Consider using a password manager to generate and store your passwords securely. These tools can help you keep track of your credentials without relying on easily forgettable passwords or writing them down on paper.

Enable two-factor authentication (2FA) whenever possible. 2FA adds an extra layer of security by requiring you to provide a second form of verification, such as a temporary code sent to your mobile device, in addition to your password. This significantly reduces the risk of unauthorized access to your accounts.

Keep Software and Devices Updated

Software and device manufacturers regularly release updates and security patches to address vulnerabilities and protect against emerging threats. It's crucial to keep your operating system, applications, and antivirus software up-to-date. Cybercriminals often exploit known vulnerabilities in outdated software, making updates a critical aspect of online security.

Set your devices and applications to automatically install updates whenever possible. This will ensure you're always running the latest, most secure versions.

Be Cautious with Personal Information

Limit the amount of personal information you share online, especially on social media platforms. Cybercriminals can use seemingly innocuous details to piece together a comprehensive profile of you, making it easier for them to carry out targeted attacks.

Review your privacy settings on social media platforms and restrict access to your personal information to only trusted contacts. Be mindful of what you post and share, as even seemingly harmless information can be used against you.

Use Encryption

Encryption is a powerful tool for protecting your online privacy. It ensures that your data is scrambled and can only be deciphered by authorized parties. Here are some ways to incorporate encryption into your online activities:

> Use secure, encrypted messaging apps for private conversations.
> Enable encryption on your email accounts, and consider using end-to-end encrypted email services.
> Use a virtual private network (VPN) when browsing the internet to encrypt your internet traffic and hide your IP address from prying eyes. A VPN is a technology that provides a secure and encrypted connection over the internet, allowing users to protect their online privacy and data by masking their IP address and routing their internet traffic through remote servers located in different geographic locations.

Beware of Phishing Attempts

Phishing attacks involve tricking individuals into revealing sensitive information, such as login credentials or financial details, by impersonating a trustworthy entity. These attacks often come in the form of deceptive emails, websites, or messages.

To protect yourself from phishing attempts:

> Be cautious when clicking on links or downloading attachments from unknown sources.
> Verify the authenticity of emails or messages from organizations requesting sensitive information.
> Educate yourself and others about common phishing tactics to recognize and avoid them.

Secure Your Wi-Fi Network

Your home Wi-Fi network is a gateway to your online world. Ensure it's secure by following these guidelines:

➢ Change the default password for your router.
➢ Enable WPA3 encryption (Wi-Fi Protected Access 3) for your Wi-Fi network.
➢ Use a strong and unique network name (SSID - Service Set Identifier) that doesn't reveal personal information.
➢ Regularly update your router's firmware to patch security vulnerabilities.

Practice Safe Online Shopping

Online shopping is convenient, but it can also expose your financial information to potential risks. To shop safely online:

➢ Only make purchases from reputable websites.
➢ Look for the padlock symbol and "https://" in the URL to confirm a secure connection.
➢ Avoid saving your credit card information on shopping websites unless absolutely necessary.
➢ Monitor your bank statements for any unauthorized transactions.

Be Wary of Public Wi-Fi

Using public Wi-Fi networks can be risky, as they are often less secure than your home network. When connecting to public Wi-Fi:

➢ Avoid accessing sensitive accounts or conducting financial transactions.
➢ Use a VPN to encrypt your internet connection.
➢ Forget the network after use to prevent automatic reconnection.

Regularly Back Up Your Data

Data loss can occur due to various reasons, including hardware failures, malware attacks, or accidental deletion. Regularly back up your important data to a secure location, such as an external hard drive or a cloud storage service. This ensures that you can recover your data even if your devices are compromised.

Monitor Your Online Presence

Regularly monitor your online presence by conducting web searches on your name and personal information. This can help you identify any unauthorized use of your data or online impersonation. If you discover any concerning information, take appropriate steps to address it.

Conclusion

Protecting your online privacy is an ongoing process that requires vigilance and awareness of potential threats. By implementing the tips mentioned in this article, you can significantly reduce the risk of falling victim to blackmail and other online threats. Remember that safeguarding your personal information is not only a matter of personal security but also a fundamental aspect of preserving your digital identity in an increasingly interconnected world. Stay informed, stay vigilant, and stay safe online.

Introduction

In today's digital age, social media has become an integral part of our lives. It allows us to connect with friends and family, share our experiences, and even build professional networks. However, with the increasing prevalence of cyber threats and online harassment, it's essential to prioritize the safety of our social media accounts and personal data. In this article, we'll explore various strategies and best practices to safeguard your online presence and protect yourself from blackmail and online threats.

Strong Passwords: The First Line of Defense

Your password is your first line of defense against unauthorized access to your social media accounts. Creating strong, unique passwords is crucial. Avoid using easily guessable information like birthdays or common phrases. Instead, opt for a combination of upper and lower-case letters, numbers, and special characters. Consider using a passphrase – a longer, memorable sequence of words or sentences – for added security. Also, avoid using the same password across multiple accounts. Utilize a reputable password manager to generate and store complex passwords securely.

Enable Two-Factor Authentication (2FA)

Two-Factor Authentication (2FA) adds an extra layer of security to your social media accounts. When you enable 2FA, you'll need to provide a second verification method, typically something you have (like a smartphone) in addition to your password. This ensures that even if someone guesses your password, they won't be able to access your account without the second factor. Many social media platforms offer 2FA options, such as sending a verification code to your mobile device or using authentication apps like Google Authenticator or Authy.

Regularly Update and Monitor Privacy Settings

Social media platforms frequently update their privacy settings and options. It's essential to stay informed about these changes and adjust your settings accordingly. Review your privacy settings regularly to ensure you're comfortable with the level of information you're sharing. Limit the visibility of your posts and personal information to only trusted friends or followers. Additionally, be cautious about granting third-party apps access to your social media accounts and review and revoke access for apps you no longer use or trust.

Beware of Phishing Attempts

Phishing is a common method used by cybercriminals to steal login credentials and personal information. Be cautious of unsolicited emails, messages, or links that ask for your login information. Legitimate social media platforms will never request your password through email or direct messages. Always verify the sender's identity and check the website's URL for authenticity before entering any sensitive information. If in doubt, contact the social media platform directly through their official channels.

Regularly Update and Patch Devices

Ensure that the devices you use to access social media are regularly updated with the latest operating system and security patches. Cybercriminals often exploit vulnerabilities in outdated software to gain access to your accounts. Set your devices to automatically update, or regularly check for updates and install them promptly. Additionally, install and maintain reputable antivirus and anti-malware software to protect against potential threats.

Be Cautious with Personal Information

While social media encourages sharing, exercise caution when disclosing personal information. Avoid sharing sensitive details such as your home address, phone number, or financial information in public posts or direct messages. Cybercriminals can use this information for various malicious purposes, including identity theft and blackmail. Think twice before sharing personal information and limit it to trusted contacts whenever possible.

Recognize and Report Harassment and Cyberbullying

Online harassment and cyberbullying are serious issues that can impact your mental and emotional well-being. Familiarize yourself with the reporting and blocking features provided by social media platforms. If you experience harassment or witness it happening to others, report the offending accounts to the platform administrators. Additionally, consider seeking support from trusted friends, family, or mental health professionals if you're dealing with the emotional toll of online harassment.

Be Wary of Public Wi-Fi

Public Wi-Fi networks are convenient but can be risky when it comes to online security. Avoid logging into your social media accounts or accessing sensitive information while connected to public Wi-Fi networks, as they may lack adequate security measures. If you must use public

Wi-Fi, consider using a Virtual Private Network (VPN) to encrypt your internet connection and protect your data from potential eavesdroppers.

Regularly Review Your Friend/Follower List

It's a good practice to review your friend or follower list on social media periodically. Remove or block individuals who you no longer wish to have access to your content or those who engage in inappropriate or harassing behavior. Additionally, be cautious about accepting friend requests from unknown or suspicious profiles, as they may have ulterior motives.

Educate Yourself and Others

One of the most effective ways to protect yourself from online threats is through education. Stay informed about the latest cybersecurity trends, scams, and social engineering tactics. Share this knowledge with your friends and family to help protect them as well. Encourage open discussions about online safety and provide resources for reporting and dealing with online threats.

Conclusion

Social media is a powerful tool for connecting with others and sharing our lives, but it also comes with risks. Safeguarding your social media accounts and personal data is essential to protect yourself from blackmail and online threats. By following these best practices, such as using strong passwords, enabling 2FA, and being cautious with personal information, you can enjoy the benefits of social media while minimizing the risks. Stay vigilant, stay informed, and remember that your online safety is in your hands.

Introduction

In today's digital age, email remains one of the most ubiquitous forms of communication. It's a tool used by individuals, businesses, and organizations worldwide for sharing information, collaborating, and conducting transactions. However, this widespread use also makes email one of the primary targets for cybercriminals. Phishing attacks, malware distribution, and various email-based threats pose significant risks to our personal and professional lives. In this article, we will delve into the world of email security and explore strategies to prevent phishing and other email-based threats.

Understanding the Threat Landscape

1. The Evolution of Email Threats

Email threats have come a long way since the days of simple spam messages. Today, cybercriminals employ sophisticated techniques to trick recipients into revealing sensitive information or downloading malicious content. Phishing, spear-phishing, and Business Email Compromise (BEC) attacks are just a few examples of these evolving threats. Phishing attacks, in particular, have become alarmingly convincing, often mimicking legitimate organizations to deceive users.

Phishing is a cyberattack technique where malicious actors use deceptive emails, websites, or messages to trick individuals into divulging sensitive information, such as login credentials, financial data, or personal details. *Spear-phishing* is a targeted form of phishing where cybercriminals craft highly personalized and deceptive messages to trick specific individuals or organizations into revealing sensitive information or taking malicious actions. *Business Email Compromise* (BEC) is a type of cyberattack in which attackers use social engineering or email spoofing techniques to impersonate high-ranking employees, executives, or trusted entities within a company. They manipulate victims into transferring funds, sharing sensitive information, or taking other actions that harm the organization, often resulting in financial losses or data breaches.

2. The High Stakes of Email Security

The consequences of email-based threats can be severe. They can result in financial loss, data breaches, identity theft, and damage to an individual or organization's reputation. Cybercriminals target individuals for personal gain, while businesses can suffer financial losses, legal repercussions, and damage to customer trust. Therefore, it's essential to implement robust email security measures.

Email Security Strategies

1. User Awareness and Training

One of the most effective email security strategies is educating users about the risks associated with email threats. Employees and individuals should be aware of the various tactics employed by cybercriminals and be able to recognize phishing attempts. Regular training sessions and awareness campaigns can empower users to make informed decisions when dealing with emails.

2. Strong Password Policies

Passwords are often the first line of defense against unauthorized access to email accounts. Encourage the use of strong, unique passwords that are difficult to guess. Implement multi-factor authentication (MFA) wherever possible, which adds an extra layer of security by requiring users to provide additional verification beyond a password.

3. Email Authentication Protocols

Implement email authentication protocols like SPF (Sender Policy Framework), DKIM (DomainKeys Identified Mail), and DMARC (Domain-based Message Authentication, Reporting, and Conformance). These protocols help verify the authenticity of incoming emails and prevent email spoofing.

SPF is an email authentication protocol that helps prevent email spoofing by specifying which mail servers are authorized to send emails on behalf of a domain. DKIM is an email authentication method that adds a digital signature to email messages to verify their authenticity and integrity. DMARC is an email authentication and reporting protocol that combines SPF and DKIM to provide stronger email security and reporting capabilities, helping to protect against email fraud and abuse.

4. Email Filtering and Anti-Malware Solutions

Deploy robust email filtering and anti-malware solutions to automatically detect and quarantine suspicious emails. These solutions can help prevent phishing emails and block attachments containing malware or ransomware. Regularly update and maintain these tools to stay ahead of evolving threats.

5. Email Encryption

Encrypting sensitive information in emails ensures that even if an email falls into the wrong hands, the content remains unreadable. Use secure email protocols like Transport Layer Security (TLS) to encrypt emails in transit. Additionally, consider end-to-end encryption for highly confidential communications.

Transport Layer Security (TLS) is a cryptographic protocol that ensures secure communication over a network, typically the internet, by encrypting data to protect it from eavesdropping and tampering. It is commonly used to secure data transmission in activities like web browsing, email, and online transactions.

6. Regular Software Updates

Cybercriminals often exploit vulnerabilities in email clients and servers to launch attacks. To mitigate this risk, keep all email-related software up to date with the latest security patches and updates. Regularly monitor for vulnerabilities and apply fixes promptly.

7. Employee Access Control

Limit access to sensitive information within the organization. Employees should have access only to the data necessary for their roles. Implement role-based access control (RBAC) to ensure that employees can access only the resources and information they need to perform their tasks. RBAC is a security model that restricts system access to authorized users based on their roles and responsibilities within an organization, ensuring that individuals only have access to the resources necessary for their specific tasks.

8. Incident Response Plan

Prepare for the possibility of a security incident. Develop a comprehensive incident response plan that outlines steps to take in case of a breach or email-based threat. Timely detection and response can minimize the damage caused by such incidents.

9. Secure Mobile Device Usage

With the increasing use of mobile devices for email communication, it's crucial to secure these devices as well. Enforce security policies on mobile devices, including encryption, remote wipe capabilities, and the use of trusted email applications.

10. Data Backup and Recovery

Regularly back up critical data and emails to ensure that, in the event of a cyberattack, you can recover lost information without paying a ransom. Implement a robust data backup and recovery strategy to safeguard against data loss.

11. Third-Party Risk Management

Evaluate the security practices of third-party vendors and partners who have access to your email systems or exchange information via email. Ensure that they adhere to email security best practices to prevent potential breaches originating from external sources.

12. Phishing Simulation and Testing

Regularly conduct phishing simulation exercises to test your organization's preparedness and the effectiveness of your training programs. Simulated phishing emails can help identify areas where users may be susceptible to attacks.

13. Continuous Monitoring and Analysis

Implement real-time monitoring and analysis of email traffic to detect anomalies and suspicious patterns. Advanced threat detection systems can help identify potential threats before they escalate into full-blown attacks.

Conclusion

Email security is a critical aspect of safeguarding individuals and organizations from the ever-evolving threats that exist in the digital world. Phishing and email-based threats continue to be lucrative avenues for cybercriminals, but with the right strategies in place, you can significantly reduce the risk of falling victim to these attacks.

Remember that email security is an ongoing process. Cybercriminals adapt to new technologies and security measures, so it's essential to stay vigilant and continuously update your email security practices. By educating users, implementing robust security measures, and maintaining a proactive stance, you can protect your personal and professional information from the ever-present threat of email-based attacks.

Introduction

In today's interconnected world, where information flows freely across digital networks, the importance of cybersecurity cannot be overstated. As individuals, businesses, and governments rely more heavily on the internet for communication, commerce, and data storage, the need to safeguard sensitive information from cyber threats has become a critical concern. In this article, we will explore the fundamentals of online security, offering insights and practical advice to help individuals and organizations protect themselves from cyber threats. By understanding these cybersecurity basics, you can better safeguard your digital assets and personal information, reducing the risk of falling victim to blackmail and other online threats.

Understanding Cyber Threats

Before delving into the specifics of cybersecurity, it's essential to comprehend the various cyber threats that exist in today's digital landscape. Cyber threats come in many forms, including:

Malware: Malicious software, such as viruses, worms, Trojans, and ransomware, designed to compromise computer systems and steal data.

Phishing: Deceptive emails or websites that trick individuals into revealing sensitive information, like login credentials or financial details.

Social Engineering: Manipulative tactics used by cybercriminals to exploit human psychology and gain unauthorized access to systems or information.

Data Breaches: Incidents where cyber attackers infiltrate a network and steal sensitive data, often for financial gain or identity theft.

Denial of Service (DoS) Attacks: Overloading a network or website to make it inaccessible to legitimate users.

Insider Threats: Security risks posed by individuals within an organization who misuse their access privileges for malicious purposes.

The Importance of Strong Passwords

One of the most fundamental aspects of online security is the use of strong passwords. Weak or easily guessable passwords are an open invitation to cybercriminals. Here are some key considerations for creating strong passwords:

Length and Complexity: Passwords should be at least 12 characters long and include a mix of upper and lower-case letters, numbers, and special characters.

Avoiding Common Words and Patterns: Refrain from using easily guessable phrases, such as "password123" or "qwerty" (keyboard layout, named after the first six letters in the top row of keys). Also, avoid patterns like "123456" or "abcdef."

Unique for Each Account: Use a different password for each online account to prevent a breach of one account compromising others.

Password Managers: Consider using a password manager to generate and securely store complex passwords for your various accounts.

Two-Factor Authentication (2FA)

Two-factor authentication (2FA) provides an additional layer of security beyond passwords. It typically involves something you know (your password) and something you have (a mobile device or hardware token). When enabled, 2FA requires users to enter a one-time code sent to their mobile device or generated by an app, making it significantly more challenging for unauthorized individuals to access your accounts.

Software Updates and Patch Management

Keeping your software up to date is critical for cybersecurity. Software developers regularly release updates and patches to fix vulnerabilities and bugs. Cybercriminals often exploit outdated software to gain access to systems. Ensure that your operating system, web browsers, antivirus software, and all applications are kept current with the latest updates and security patches.

Firewalls and Network Security

Firewalls act as a barrier between your computer and the internet, filtering incoming and outgoing network traffic. They can be either hardware or software-based and are essential for safeguarding your device from unauthorized access and malicious software. Additionally, consider implementing network security measures like intrusion detection systems (IDS) and intrusion prevention systems (IPS) to monitor network traffic and detect potential threats. IDS is a security tool that monitors network or system activities for signs of malicious or unauthorized behavior and issues alerts when such activities are detected. IPS is a security tool that not only detects suspicious activities but also actively blocks or mitigates potential threats to prevent unauthorized access or malicious behavior in real-time.

Email Security

Email is a common vector for cyberattacks, particularly phishing attempts. To enhance email security:

Be cautious of unsolicited emails: Don't click on links or download attachments from unknown sources.

Verify email senders: Ensure that the sender's email address matches the legitimate domain of the organization they claim to represent.

Use email filtering: Enable spam filters to reduce the number of phishing emails that reach your inbox.

Data Encryption

Data encryption is the process of converting data into a code to prevent unauthorized access. It ensures that even if data is intercepted, it remains unreadable to unauthorized parties. Employ encryption for sensitive information, both in transit (e.g., during online transactions) and at rest (e.g., on your hard drive or cloud storage).

Regular Backups

Regularly backing up your data is a critical aspect of cybersecurity. In the event of a ransomware attack or data breach, having up-to-date backups can save you from losing valuable information. Store backups in a secure location, preferably offline, to prevent them from being compromised during a cyberattack.

Employee Training and Awareness

In organizations, employees can be both a cybersecurity asset and a vulnerability. Providing cybersecurity training and promoting awareness among employees is essential to prevent insider threats and ensure best practices are followed. Training should cover topics such as recognizing phishing attempts, practicing secure password management, and reporting security incidents promptly.

Incident Response Plan

No cybersecurity strategy is complete without an incident response plan. This plan outlines the steps to take in the event of a cyber incident and helps minimize damage and downtime. It should include procedures for identifying and containing the breach, notifying affected parties, and recovering compromised systems.

Vendor and Third-Party Risk Management

Many organizations rely on third-party vendors and service providers for various functions. However, these relationships can introduce security risks. It's crucial to assess and manage the cybersecurity practices of vendors and third parties to ensure they meet your security standards. This may include contractually obligating them to maintain a certain level of security.

Continuous Monitoring and Threat Intelligence

Cyber threats evolve rapidly, so continuous monitoring and threat intelligence are essential. Stay informed about emerging threats, vulnerabilities, and attack trends. Invest in security tools and services that provide real-time monitoring and alerts to detect and respond to threats promptly.

Legal and Regulatory Compliance

Compliance with cybersecurity laws and regulations is not just a legal requirement but also a fundamental part of online security. Understand the applicable laws in your industry and region, and ensure your cybersecurity practices align with these requirements.

Conclusion

Cybersecurity is an ever-evolving field, and staying ahead of cyber threats requires continuous effort and vigilance. By understanding and implementing these cybersecurity basics, individuals and organizations can significantly reduce their risk of falling victim to blackmail and other online threats. Remember that cybersecurity is not a one-time task but an ongoing commitment to protecting digital assets, sensitive information, and personal privacy in an increasingly digital world.

Introduction

In an era where the digital landscape is expanding exponentially, the need for robust cybersecurity measures has never been greater. With the rise of online threats, data breaches, and cyberattacks, individuals and organizations must arm themselves with the right tools and software to protect their sensitive information and digital assets. This article explores a range of cybersecurity tools designed to safeguard against blackmail and online threats, empowering users to defend themselves in the ever-evolving digital battleground.

Antivirus Software: Your First Line of Defense

Antivirus software has long been the cornerstone of cybersecurity. It serves as the first line of defense against a multitude of online threats, including viruses, malware, ransomware, and spyware. These programs employ signature-based detection to identify and quarantine malicious files, preventing them from infecting your system. Some renowned antivirus solutions include Norton, McAfee, Kaspersky, and Bitdefender.

However, in the age of advanced threats, modern antivirus software goes beyond traditional signature-based scanning. It utilizes heuristic analysis, behavior monitoring, and artificial intelligence to detect and block emerging threats that may not have known signatures. Keeping your antivirus software up-to-date is crucial, as it ensures protection against the latest threats.

Firewalls: Safeguarding Your Digital Perimeter

Firewalls act as gatekeepers for your network, filtering incoming and outgoing traffic to protect against unauthorized access and cyberattacks. They come in two primary forms: hardware and software.

Hardware Firewalls: These are typically deployed at the network level, protecting an entire network from external threats. They are often integrated into routers and are highly effective at blocking unwanted traffic.

Software Firewalls: These are installed on individual devices and provide granular control over incoming and outgoing traffic. They allow users to define rules for specific applications and services, providing an added layer of security.

Popular firewall solutions include Windows Firewall for individual devices and dedicated hardware firewalls like Cisco ASA and Fortinet FortiGate for network-level protection.

Virtual Private Networks (VPNs): Securing Your Online Privacy

In an age of surveillance and data tracking, VPNs have become essential tools for safeguarding online privacy. A VPN encrypts your internet connection, making it difficult for hackers, advertisers, or government agencies to monitor your online activities. It also masks your IP address, making it appear as though you're browsing from a different location.

When choosing a VPN service, look for one that offers robust encryption, a strict no-logs policy, and a large server network to ensure anonymity and high-speed browsing. Notable VPN providers include ExpressVPN, NordVPN, and CyberGhost.

Password Managers: Enhancing Password Security

Weak passwords are a common vulnerability exploited by cybercriminals. Password managers address this issue by generating strong, unique passwords for each of your online accounts and storing them securely. They also autofill login credentials, reducing the risk of falling victim to phishing attacks.

Password managers use encryption to protect your data, and many offer features such as two-factor authentication (2FA) for added security. Popular choices include LastPass, Dashlane, and 1Password.

Multi-Factor Authentication (MFA): Adding an Extra Layer of Security

Even the strongest password can be compromised, which is why multi-factor authentication (MFA) is crucial. MFA requires users to provide two or more forms of identification before granting access, typically something they know (password) and something they have (e.g., a mobile device).

MFA can be implemented using various methods, including SMS codes, authenticator apps like Google Authenticator or Authy, and hardware tokens. Enabling MFA across your online accounts provides an additional layer of protection against unauthorized access.

Intrusion Detection Systems (IDS) and Intrusion Prevention Systems (IPS)

Intrusion Detection Systems (IDS) and Intrusion Prevention Systems (IPS) are critical tools for identifying and mitigating network threats. These systems monitor network traffic for suspicious activity and patterns, such as unusual access attempts or known attack signatures.

IDS: IDS passively monitor network traffic and generate alerts when they detect potential threats. They do not take direct action to block threats but provide valuable insights for administrators to investigate.

IPS: IPS, on the other hand, actively intervene to block suspicious traffic or attacks in real-time. They can automatically apply predefined security policies to mitigate threats.

Snort and Suricata are popular open-source IDS/IPS solutions, while commercial options include Cisco Firepower and Palo Alto Networks.

Email Security Software: Defending Against Phishing Attacks

Phishing attacks remain a prevalent threat, and email is a common vector for such attacks. Email security software is designed to filter out malicious emails, spam, and phishing attempts, reducing the risk of falling victim to social engineering attacks.

These tools often employ machine learning algorithms and email authentication protocols to identify and block phishing emails. Leading email security solutions include Proofpoint, Barracuda, and Mimecast.

Endpoint Detection and Response (EDR) Solutions

With the increasing sophistication of cyber threats, endpoint security has become a critical component of cybersecurity. EDR solutions are designed to detect, investigate, and respond to advanced threats targeting individual devices (endpoints) within a network.

EDR tools continuously monitor endpoints for suspicious behavior, such as unauthorized access or unusual file activity. They also provide threat hunting capabilities and incident response workflows. Notable EDR solutions include CrowdStrike Falcon, Carbon Black, and SentinelOne.

Web Application Firewalls (WAFs): Protecting Web-Based Assets

Web applications are frequent targets for cyberattacks, making Web Application Firewalls (WAFs) essential for protecting them. A WAF filters incoming web traffic, identifying and blocking malicious requests and attacks like SQL injection, cross-site scripting (XSS), and distributed denial of service (DDoS) attacks.

SQL injection is a type of cyberattack where malicious SQL code is inserted into input fields of a web application, exploiting vulnerabilities to manipulate a database and potentially gain unauthorized access or steal data. XSS is a web security vulnerability that allows attackers to inject malicious scripts into webpages viewed by other users, potentially leading to data theft or manipulation. DDoS attacks involve overwhelming a target system, service, or network with a flood of traffic from multiple sources, rendering it inaccessible to legitimate users. These attacks disrupt services and often aim to disrupt or temporarily disable online services.

WAFs come in various deployment options, including cloud-based and on-premises solutions. Some popular choices include Cloudflare WAF, Imperva WAF, and Akamai Kona Site Defender.

Security Information and Event Management (SIEM) Systems

SIEM systems play a vital role in cybersecurity by collecting, correlating, and analyzing data from various sources across an organization's IT infrastructure. They help identify security incidents, provide real-time monitoring, and facilitate compliance reporting.

SIEM platforms like Splunk, LogRhythm, and IBM QRadar offer features such as log management, incident detection, and threat intelligence integration. They are especially valuable for enterprises and organizations with complex IT environments.

Data Encryption Tools: Protecting Sensitive Information

Data encryption is essential for safeguarding sensitive information, both in transit and at rest. Encryption tools use algorithms to convert data into an unreadable format, which can only be deciphered with the correct decryption key.

File Encryption: File encryption tools like VeraCrypt and BitLocker allow users to encrypt specific files or entire disk drives, ensuring that unauthorized users cannot access the data.

Communication Encryption: Secure communication is achieved through protocols like HTTPS for web browsing and end-to-end encryption in messaging apps like Signal and WhatsApp.

Email Encryption: Tools like PGP (Pretty Good Privacy) and S/MIME can be used to encrypt email messages, protecting the contents from eavesdroppers.

Security Awareness Training: Educating Users

No cybersecurity tool is complete without educated users who understand the risks and best practices. Security awareness training programs teach individuals how to recognize and respond to potential threats, such as phishing emails, social engineering, and safe web browsing.

These programs often include simulated phishing exercises and provide ongoing education to keep users informed about emerging threats.

Conclusion

In today's digital age, safeguarding against blackmail and online threats is a top priority. A comprehensive cybersecurity strategy requires a combination of tools and software to protect against a diverse range of threats. From antivirus software and firewalls to VPNs, password managers, and advanced threat detection systems, these tools are essential in the ongoing battle against cybercriminals.

Remember that cybersecurity is not a one-time effort but an ongoing process. Regularly update your software, educate yourself and your team about the latest threats, and continually assess and enhance your cybersecurity measures. By staying vigilant and leveraging the right cybersecurity tools, individuals and organizations can better protect themselves from the ever-evolving landscape of online threats.

Introduction

In the digital age, where we conduct a significant portion of our lives online, safeguarding our personal information from cyber threats is of paramount importance. One of the first lines of defense in this battle is password management. Passwords are the keys to our digital kingdom, and creating strong and unique passwords is the cornerstone of protecting ourselves from blackmail and online threats. In this article, we will explore various strategies for crafting robust passwords that can withstand even the most determined attackers.

The Importance of Strong and Unique Passwords

Before delving into the strategies for creating strong and unique passwords, it's crucial to understand why they are so essential in today's digital landscape.

Protecting Personal Data: Strong passwords act as a shield against unauthorized access to your personal data, including financial information, private communications, and sensitive documents.

Preventing Identity Theft: Cybercriminals can use stolen passwords to impersonate you, potentially leading to identity theft and fraud.

Safeguarding Online Accounts: Your online accounts, from social media to email and banking, are only as secure as your passwords. A weak password can lead to unauthorized access and misuse of these accounts.

: **By creating strong passwords, you** can thwart various cyberattacks, such as brute-force attacks and dictionary attacks, which rely on guessing or systematically trying different combinations.

Brute-force attacks are a type of cyberattack where an attacker systematically tries all possible combinations of passwords or encryption keys until the correct one is found, allowing unauthorized access to a system, account, or data. These attacks are time-consuming but can be effective if passwords are weak or not properly protected. Dictionary attacks are a type of cyberattack in which an attacker systematically tries a list of words, phrases, or commonly used passwords in an attempt to gain unauthorized access to a system, account, or data. These attacks exploit weak or easily guessable passwords by testing a predefined set of possibilities.

Protecting Against Blackmail: **Strong and unique** passwords help safeguard your online presence, making it more challenging for malicious individuals to gain access to compromising information that could be used for blackmail.

Now that we understand the significance of strong and unique passwords, let's explore effective strategies for creating and managing them.

Strategies for Creating Strong and Unique Passwords

1. Length Matters: Go Long

When it comes to password strength, size matters. Longer passwords are inherently more secure than shorter ones. Aim for a minimum of 12 characters, and consider using even longer passwords when possible. Longer passwords provide more combinations, making them harder to crack.

2. Use a Mix of Characters

To enhance password complexity, use a combination of different character types:

- ❖ Uppercase Letters: Include at least one uppercase letter.
- ❖ Lowercase Letters: Include at least one lowercase letter.
- ❖ Numbers: Incorporate numbers, but avoid obvious choices like "12345."
- ❖ Special Symbols: Use special characters like @, #, $, or % to add an extra layer of complexity.

3. Avoid Common Words and Phrases

Hackers often use dictionaries and lists of common passwords to crack accounts. Avoid using easily guessable words, such as "password," "admin," or common phrases like "iloveyou". Also, steer clear of easily discoverable personal information like your name, birthdate, or pet's name.

4. Randomness is Key

Generate random sequences of characters for your passwords rather than using easily guessable patterns. Avoid consecutive or repeating characters, such as "aaaaaa" or "12345."

5. Passphrases: The Power of Length and Unpredictability

Consider using passphrases – longer, memorable sentences or combinations of words. These can be both strong and unique. For example, "PurpleLion$JumpedHigh" is a strong passphrase that is also easy to remember.

6. Avoid Using the Same Password Across Multiple Sites

Reusing passwords across different websites is a common and dangerous practice. If one of your accounts is compromised, it could lead to a domino effect of breaches. Use a unique password for each account.

7. Password Managers: Your Digital Vault

Managing numerous strong and unique passwords can be challenging, but password managers can simplify the process. They securely store your passwords and generate strong, random passwords for you. Popular password managers include LastPass, 1Password, and Dashlane.

8. Two-Factor Authentication (2FA)

Implement two-factor authentication wherever possible. This adds an extra layer of security by requiring a secondary verification method, such as a code sent to your mobile device or email, in addition to your password.

9. Regularly Update Passwords

Change your passwords periodically, even if there's no apparent security breach. This practice ensures that if a password is compromised, it won't remain useful for long.

10. Beware of Phishing Attempts

Be cautious of phishing emails and websites that attempt to trick you into revealing your login credentials. Always verify the legitimacy of a website before entering your password.

11. Educate Yourself and Stay Informed

Stay up-to-date with the latest security practices and emerging threats. Cybersecurity is an evolving field, and what is secure today may not be tomorrow.

Conclusion

In an era where the digital realm plays an increasingly significant role in our lives, safeguarding our online presence is paramount. Strong and unique passwords are the first line of defense against blackmail and online threats. By following the strategies outlined in this article, you can significantly enhance your online security.

Remember that creating and managing strong passwords is an ongoing process. Regularly update your passwords, employ the use of a trusted password manager, and be vigilant against phishing attempts. By taking these precautions, you can fortify your digital defenses and minimize the risk of falling victim to cyber threats. Protect your online identity and personal data – your digital well-being depends on it.

Introduction

In our increasingly digital world, the threat of online threats and cyberattacks is ever-present. Blackmail and other malicious activities have become more sophisticated, targeting individuals and organizations alike. To safeguard oneself from such threats, it is essential to implement robust security measures, and one of the most effective tools in this regard is Two-Factor Authentication (2FA). In this article, we will explore what 2FA is, why it's crucial, and how to enable it for added security.

Understanding Two-Factor Authentication (2FA)

1. What is 2FA?

Two-Factor Authentication (2FA) is a security process that requires users to provide two different authentication factors before gaining access to an account or system. These factors typically fall into three categories:

Something you know: This could be a password, PIN, or security questions.

Something you have: This includes a smartphone, hardware token, or smart card.

Something you are: Biometric data like fingerprint or facial recognition.

By combining two of these factors, 2FA significantly enhances security compared to relying solely on a password.

Passwords, while ubiquitous, are inherently vulnerable. They can be easily stolen, guessed, or cracked by determined attackers. With the proliferation of data breaches, where millions of passwords are exposed, relying solely on a password is akin to leaving the front door of your digital life wide open.

The Importance of Enabling 2FA

1. Mitigating the Risk of Blackmail

Blackmail is a malicious act where cybercriminals threaten to disclose sensitive or embarrassing information unless a victim complies with their demands. Enabling 2FA on your accounts adds an extra layer of security that can make it incredibly difficult for attackers to gain unauthorized access to your personal information or online profiles.

2. Preventing Unauthorized Access

Even if you're not a high-profile target for blackmail, unauthorized access to your accounts can have severe consequences. From email accounts to social media profiles and financial services, unauthorized access can lead to identity theft, financial losses, and reputational damage. 2FA serves as a barrier against such intrusions.

Enabling Two-Factor Authentication (2FA)

Now that we understand the importance of 2FA, let's explore the general process of enabling it on different platforms and services. Please note that specific steps may vary due to updates by service providers.

1. Social Media Accounts

Social media accounts are often targeted by cybercriminals due to the wealth of personal information they contain.

Access your account settings: Log in to your social media account (Facebook, Twitter, Instagram etc.), navigate to account settings, and locate the security or privacy section.

Enable 2FA: Look for the 2FA option and follow the on-screen instructions to enable it, choosing your preferred method.

2. Email Accounts

Email accounts serve as gateways to much of your online presence, so securing them is crucial.

Access your email's security settings: Log in to your email account (Gmail, Outlook/Hotmail etc.), find the security settings section, and look for 2FA options.

Enable 2FA: Follow the instructions provided to enable 2FA using your chosen method.

3. Financial Services

Protecting your financial accounts is essential to prevent identity theft and financial losses.

Visit your provider: Access your bank or financial service provider's website or contact customer support to inquire about 2FA options.

Enable 2FA: Follow the provided instructions to enable 2FA for your financial accounts.

4. Online Shopping

Online shopping accounts often store sensitive payment information.

Access your account settings: Log in to your online shopping account (Amazon, eBay etc.), access account settings, and look for security or privacy options.

Enable 2FA: Follow the instructions to enable 2FA, selecting your preferred method.

5. Cloud Services

Cloud services store valuable data, making them attractive targets.

Access your cloud service settings: Log in to your cloud service account (Dropbox, Google Drive etc.), navigate to settings, and search for security or 2FA options.

Enable 2FA: Follow the provided instructions to enable 2FA using your chosen method.

6. Gaming Platforms

Gaming accounts are valuable and may link to payment methods and in-game items.

Access your gaming account settings: Log in to your gaming platform account (Steam, Xbox Live/PlayStation Network etc.) and find the security or privacy settings.

Enable 2FA: Follow the on-screen instructions to enable 2FA, selecting your preferred method.

Remember to keep your 2FA method secure and do not share your codes or authentication app with anyone. This added security layer helps protect your accounts from unauthorized access.

Conclusion

Two-Factor Authentication (2FA) is a simple yet highly effective way to enhance your online security. In a world where online threats and blackmail attempts are on the rise, taking proactive steps to protect your digital identity is essential. By enabling 2FA on your accounts, you create an additional layer of defense that significantly reduces the risk of unauthorized access and potential blackmail.

Remember, while 2FA greatly improves security, it's not foolproof. Staying vigilant, keeping your devices and software up to date, and regularly reviewing your online accounts for suspicious activity are all crucial components of a comprehensive cybersecurity strategy. Safeguarding yourself from blackmail and online threats requires constant attention and proactive measures, and 2FA is an excellent place to start.

Chapter 13. Protecting Personal Documents

Introduction

In today's digital age, safeguarding our personal documents has become more critical than ever. As we increasingly store sensitive information digitally and share documents online, we expose ourselves to potential threats like blackmail and online attacks. This article aims to provide comprehensive guidance on how to protect your personal documents effectively, ensuring that your sensitive information remains secure. By following these strategies, you can minimize the risk of falling victim to blackmail and online threats.

Understanding the Value of Personal Documents

Before delving into the strategies for protecting personal documents, it's essential to understand the value of these documents. Personal documents often contain information such as financial records, medical history, legal documents, and personal correspondence. This information is invaluable to cybercriminals, identity thieves, and potential blackmailers. Recognizing the worth of your personal documents is the first step in ensuring their protection.

The Importance of Digital Security

In the digital age, most of our personal documents are stored electronically. Therefore, robust digital security is crucial to safeguarding sensitive information.

1. Passwords and Authentication

Use strong, unique passwords for all your accounts, and avoid easily guessable information like birthdays or common phrases. Enable two-factor authentication (2FA) wherever possible to add an extra layer of security. Consider using a reputable password manager to generate and store complex passwords securely.

2. Encryption

Encrypt your sensitive files and folders using encryption software. Use secure messaging apps that offer end-to-end encryption for confidential conversations.

3. Regular Software Updates

Keep your operating system and software applications up-to-date with the latest security patches. Enable automatic updates to ensure you're protected against known vulnerabilities.

4. Anti-Malware Software

Install reputable anti-malware and antivirus software to detect and remove potential threats. Regularly scan your devices for malware and viruses.

5. Safe Document Storage

Even with strong digital security measures in place, it's important to store physical copies of personal documents securely.

Invest in a fireproof and waterproof home safe to store essential physical documents like passports, birth certificates, and wills. Ensure that your safe is securely bolted to the floor or wall to prevent theft.

Offsite storage refers to the practice of storing data, documents, or physical assets at a location separate from the primary place of business or residence. This is done to ensure data redundancy, disaster recovery, or simply to free up space, and it can involve using remote data centers, secure facilities, or cloud storage services to safeguard and access important information or items when needed.

Consider using a secure offsite storage facility for important documents, such as legal or financial records. Ensure that the facility has robust security measures in place, including surveillance and access controls.

Create digital copies of important physical documents and store them in a secure cloud storage service. Use strong encryption and two-factor authentication for accessing cloud storage.

Document Organization and Classification

Effective document management is crucial for security. Organize and classify your documents to ensure easy access while maintaining security.

1. Categorize Documents

Group documents into categories such as financial, medical, legal, and personal. This classification helps you locate specific documents quickly and keeps sensitive information organized.

2. Document Naming Conventions

Use clear and consistent naming conventions for digital files. Avoid using easily identifiable names that might expose the document's content.

3. Secure Labels

Label physical folders or containers with non-descriptive names to prevent outsiders from guessing their contents.

4. Secure Sharing Practices

Sharing personal documents with trusted individuals or organizations is common. However, it's essential to follow secure sharing practices.

5. Password Protection

When sharing sensitive documents electronically, password-protect the files and share the password separately. Communicate the password through a secure channel, such as a phone call or encrypted messaging app.

6. Secure Email

Use encrypted email services or encryption plugins when sending sensitive documents via email. Avoid sending sensitive information through unsecured email accounts.

7. Verify Recipients

Verify the identity of recipients before sharing sensitive documents. Confirm the recipient's contact details through a trusted source to avoid falling victim to phishing attacks.

8. Data Backup and Recovery

To protect personal documents from data loss due to unforeseen circumstances, implement a reliable data backup and recovery strategy.

9. Regular Backups

Create regular backups of your digital documents and store them in different locations, including external hard drives and cloud storage. Test your backups periodically to ensure they are functional.

10. Data Recovery Plan

Develop a data recovery plan that outlines steps to recover lost or compromised documents. Include contact information for IT support or data recovery specialists in case of emergencies.

11. Document Disposal and Shredding

Proper document disposal is just as crucial as secure storage. Dispose of sensitive documents carefully to prevent unauthorized access.

12. Shredding

Invest in a high-quality shredder to destroy physical documents containing sensitive information. Ensure that shredded documents are disposed of in a secure manner.

13. Electronic Data Wiping

Use data wiping software to securely erase data from electronic devices before disposing of them. Remove personal information from old smartphones, laptops, and hard drives.

14. Protecting Against Social Engineering

Cybercriminals often employ social engineering tactics to gain access to personal documents. Stay vigilant against.

15. Phishing Attacks

Be cautious of unsolicited emails or messages asking for personal information. Verify the legitimacy of requests for sensitive information before responding.

16. Impersonation

Confirm the identity of individuals or organizations requesting personal documents. Contact them directly through trusted channels to verify their requests.

Legal Considerations

Understanding relevant laws and regulations is essential for protecting personal documents.

1. Data Privacy Laws

Familiarize yourself with data privacy laws applicable in your region, such as the General Data Protection Regulation (GDPR) in Europe or Health Insurance Portability and Accountability Act (HIPAA) in the United States. Ensure compliance with these laws when handling personal information.

2. Legal Counsel

Seek legal counsel when dealing with complex legal documents or sensitive contracts. Ensure that you fully understand the implications of any document before signing it.

Conclusion

Protecting personal documents from threats like blackmail and online attacks requires a proactive approach. By implementing strong digital security measures, practicing safe document storage and sharing, and staying informed about legal considerations, you can significantly reduce the risk of your sensitive information falling into the wrong hands. Remember that safeguarding your personal documents is an ongoing process, and staying vigilant is key to maintaining your privacy and security in an increasingly digital world.

Introduction

In today's digital age, our lives are increasingly intertwined with the internet. While this connectivity brings numerous benefits, it also exposes us to various online threats, one of the most distressing being sextortion. Sextortion is a form of blackmail where malicious actors use sexually explicit content as leverage to manipulate and coerce victims. This article aims to shed light on the insidious nature of sextortion, provide strategies for prevention, and guidance on how to handle sextortion threats if they arise.

Understanding Sextortion

Sextortion is a heinous crime that exploits victims emotionally, psychologically, and often financially. It typically involves the following elements:

Initial Contact: The perpetrator makes contact with the victim through various means, including email, social media, or dating apps. They may pose as a potential romantic interest, often using a fake profile.

Grooming: The perpetrator builds a rapport with the victim, gaining their trust over time. They engage in conversations that gradually become more intimate, often leading to the exchange of explicit photos or videos.

Threats: Once the perpetrator possesses compromising material, they turn the tables on the victim. They threaten to expose the explicit content to the victim's friends, family, or colleagues unless certain demands are met, usually involving money or further explicit material.

Prevention Strategies

1. Maintain Privacy and Security

Strong Passwords: Use strong, unique passwords for all online accounts. Utilize a reputable password manager to keep track of them.

Two-Factor Authentication (2FA): Enable 2FA whenever possible, adding an extra layer of security to your online accounts.

Be Cautious with Personal Information: Avoid sharing personal information, such as your home address or financial details, with individuals you meet online.

2. Verify Online Identities

Be Skeptical: Exercise caution when interacting with strangers online. Verify the identities of people you connect with on social media and dating apps.

Video Calls: Suggest video calls to confirm the identity of the person you're communicating with. Fake profiles often shy away from face-to-face interactions.

3. Maintain Boundaries

Avoid Explicit Content: Refrain from sending explicit photos or videos, even if you trust the person you're talking to. Once it's out there, you lose control over it.

Trust Your Instincts: If something feels off or suspicious about an online interaction, trust your instincts and consider discontinuing communication.

4. Educate Yourself

Awareness: Educate yourself and your loved ones about the dangers of sextortion. Knowledge is a powerful tool in preventing victimization.

Resources: Familiarize yourself with resources and support networks available to help victims of sextortion.

5. Handling Sextortion Threats

If you find yourself a victim of sextortion, it's crucial to take the following steps:

Do Not Give in to Blackmail

Stay Calm: Try to remain composed and avoid panicking. The perpetrator thrives on your fear and desperation.

Cease Communication: Stop all communication with the blackmailer immediately. Do not engage further.

Do Not Pay: Refuse to meet the blackmailer's demands, whether they involve money or more explicit content. Paying will not guarantee your safety and may embolden them to demand more.

6. Document Evidence

Preserve All Messages: Save all communication with the blackmailer, including emails, messages, and any other relevant evidence.

Screenshot: Take screenshots of the threats and explicit content, if applicable. These can serve as valuable evidence later.

7. Report to Authorities

Contact Law Enforcement: Report the sextortion incident to your local law enforcement agency. Provide them with all the evidence you have gathered.

Cybercrime Units: Many jurisdictions have specialized cybercrime units equipped to handle cases like sextortion.

8. Seek Support

Talk to Someone: Share your situation with a trusted friend, family member, or therapist. Support is crucial during this challenging time.

Reach Out to Victim Support Services: Many organizations provide support and guidance to victims of online blackmail and sextortion.

9. Secure Your Online Presence

Change Passwords: Immediately change the passwords for all your online accounts to prevent further intrusion.

Adjust Privacy Settings: Review and enhance the privacy settings on your social media profiles and other online platforms.

10. Legal Recourse

Consult an Attorney: **Seek legal advice on potential legal action against the blackmailer. Laws regarding sextortion vary by jurisdiction.**

Civil Lawsuits: **Consider pursuing civil action against the perpetrator to seek damages.**

Conclusion

Sextortion is a disturbing and growing threat in the digital age, but by staying informed and taking precautions, you can reduce your risk of falling victim to it. If you do find yourself targeted by a sextortionist, remember that you are not alone, and there are resources available to help you through this difficult experience. By refusing to give in to the demands of blackmailers, documenting evidence, and seeking support, you can take steps towards reclaiming your control and safeguarding yourself from further harm. The battle against sextortion begins with awareness, prevention, and resilience, and it is a fight that we can win together.

Introduction

In an increasingly digital world, our lives are intricately woven into the fabric of the internet. From our social media profiles to online purchases, from email communications to web searches, every digital action we take leaves a trace, forming what is commonly referred to as our "digital footprint." While the digital age has brought about unparalleled convenience and connectivity, it has also raised concerns about privacy and security. This article explores the concept of digital footprint management and provides strategies to help individuals safeguard themselves from potential threats, including blackmail and online attacks.

Understanding Your Digital Footprint

1. What is a Digital Footprint?

Your digital footprint is the sum total of all the online activities and interactions you engage in. It encompasses the data you willingly share, such as social media posts and photos, as well as the information gathered about you through passive means, like cookies and tracking mechanisms on websites. Your digital footprint can be both explicit (intentionally shared data) and implicit (data collected without your explicit consent).

2. The Permanence of Digital Footprints

One crucial aspect of digital footprints is their permanence. Once something is posted or shared online, it can often be archived, shared, and accessed long after you've moved on.

This permanence poses both opportunities and risks. It allows for the sharing of knowledge and experiences but also leaves room for misuse and exploitation.

The Importance of Managing Your Digital Footprint

1. Protecting Your Privacy

Managing your digital footprint is crucial for protecting your privacy. In an era where data breaches and online threats are prevalent, safeguarding your personal information is paramount. By reducing your digital footprint, you minimize the exposure of sensitive data, making it harder for malicious actors to exploit or misuse your information.

2. Mitigating Online Threats

A well-managed digital footprint can also mitigate the risk of online threats, including blackmail. Digital attackers often exploit the information they find online to create convincing and targeted attacks. By limiting the available information, you can make it more challenging for attackers to craft credible threats.

Strategies for Minimizing Your Digital Footprint

1. Review and Cleanse Social Media Profiles

Social media platforms are one of the primary sources of personal information in the digital age. Begin your digital footprint management by reviewing and cleansing your social media profiles. Remove or limit access to sensitive personal information and regularly update your privacy settings. Consider sharing less personal information, such as your phone number or home address, on public profiles.

2. Practice Discretion in Online Sharing

Think twice before sharing personal details or intimate moments online. Understand that even seemingly harmless posts can be exploited when combined with other available information. Be cautious about sharing location data, and use discretion when posting photos that reveal your daily routines or whereabouts.

3. Regularly Update and Review Privacy Settings

Most online services provide options to adjust privacy settings. Regularly review and update these settings to ensure you have control over who can access your data. Customize your settings to limit data sharing with third parties and restrict access to your personal information.

4. Use Strong, Unique Passwords

Password security is a critical aspect of digital footprint management. Use strong, unique passwords for all your online accounts, and consider using a password manager to keep track of them. Avoid using easily guessable information, such as birthdays or names, in your passwords.

5. Enable Two-Factor Authentication (2FA)

Two-factor authentication adds an extra layer of security to your online accounts. Whenever possible, enable 2FA to ensure that even if your password is compromised, a second authentication step is required to access your account.

6. Be Wary of Public Wi-Fi

Public Wi-Fi networks can be insecure and vulnerable to hacking. Avoid conducting sensitive activities, such as online banking or accessing private accounts, on public Wi-Fi networks. If necessary, use a virtual private network (VPN) to encrypt your internet connection.

7. Limit Personal Information on E-commerce Websites

When making online purchases, only provide the essential information required for the transaction. Avoid saving credit card information on websites unless absolutely necessary. Be cautious about sharing your email address with online retailers, as it may lead to unsolicited marketing emails.

8. Regularly Clear Browsing History and Cookies

Browsers store a history of your online activities and use cookies to track your behavior. Periodically clear your browsing history and cookies to minimize the data collected about you. You can also use browser extensions that enhance your privacy by blocking trackers.

9. Be Cautious with Email and Messaging

Emails and messaging apps can be a treasure trove of personal information. Be cautious when sharing sensitive information via email, and use encrypted messaging apps for secure communications. Regularly delete old emails and messages that contain personal data.

Set up Google Alerts or use online reputation management tools to monitor mentions of your name or personal information online. This can help you identify and address any instances of personal data exposure or potential threats promptly.

Stay informed about evolving privacy risks and online threats. Knowledge is your best defense. By understanding the tactics used by cybercriminals, you can better protect yourself and your digital footprint.

Conclusion

In an era where our digital presence is both a source of connectivity and vulnerability, it's essential to take proactive steps to manage and minimize your digital footprint. By following the strategies outlined in this article, you can protect your privacy, mitigate online threats, and reduce the risk of falling victim to blackmail or other malicious activities. Remember that safeguarding your digital footprint is an ongoing process that requires vigilance and adaptability in the ever-changing landscape of the digital world.

Introduction

In our increasingly digital world, the threats of blackmail and cyberbullying have become all too common. The anonymity offered by the internet has emboldened individuals with malicious intent to target innocent people, often for personal gain or revenge. For those who find themselves facing these threats, seeking help and support is crucial to protect their well-being and take appropriate action against the perpetrators. This article explores the various resources available for individuals dealing with blackmail or cyber threats, emphasizing the importance of seeking help and taking proactive measures to safeguard oneself online.

Understanding the Threat

1. The Nature of Blackmail and Cyber Threats

Blackmail and cyber threats can take various forms, from explicit threats to release compromising photos or information to demanding money or other favors under the threat of exposure. In some cases, these threats are driven by personal vendettas, while others are motivated purely by financial gain. Understanding the nature of these threats is essential in assessing the appropriate response.

2. The Psychological Impact

Victims of blackmail and cyber threats often experience severe psychological distress. Fear, anxiety, and a sense of powerlessness can overwhelm individuals in such situations. It is crucial to acknowledge these emotions and seek support to cope effectively.

Seeking Help and Support

1. Legal Assistance

One of the first steps individuals facing blackmail or cyber threats should consider is seeking legal assistance. Depending on the nature of the threat, this could involve contacting local law enforcement or hiring an attorney with expertise in cybercrime and online harassment cases.

2. Reporting to Authorities

When faced with threats that involve illegal activities such as hacking, cyberstalking, or extortion, reporting the incidents to the appropriate authorities is crucial. This can help initiate investigations and potentially lead to the apprehension of the perpetrator. Local law enforcement agencies, as well as national cybercrime units, can provide guidance on reporting procedures.

3. Cybersecurity Measures

Prevention is key when dealing with cyber threats. Individuals should take proactive steps to secure their online presence by using strong, unique passwords, enabling two-factor authentication, and regularly updating their software and antivirus programs. Consulting cybersecurity experts can also provide valuable insights into protecting one's digital identity.

4. Online Reputation Management

For individuals who are concerned about the release of compromising information or damaging content, online reputation management services can be a helpful resource. These services work to mitigate the impact of harmful information by pushing it down in search engine results and promoting positive content.

5. Counseling and Therapy

The emotional toll of blackmail and cyber threats can be overwhelming. Seeking counseling or therapy from a qualified mental health professional can provide victims with the tools to cope with anxiety, fear, and trauma. Many therapists specialize in trauma and crisis counseling and can offer invaluable support.

6. Support Groups

Connecting with others who have experienced similar situations can be highly therapeutic. Support groups, whether in-person or online, provide a safe space for individuals to share their experiences, receive emotional support, and learn coping strategies from others who have been through similar ordeals.

7. Hotlines and Helplines

Various organizations offer hotlines and helplines specifically designed to assist victims of online harassment and cyber threats. These services provide immediate support and guidance on how to navigate the situation. They can also refer individuals to legal, psychological, or cybersecurity experts as needed.

8. Nonprofit Organizations

Several nonprofit organizations focus on helping individuals facing online threats and blackmail. These organizations offer a range of services, from legal assistance to emotional support, and often collaborate with law enforcement agencies to combat cybercrime.

9. Legal Remedies

Depending on the nature of the threats and the laws in their jurisdiction, victims may have legal remedies available to them. This could include obtaining restraining orders or filing civil lawsuits against the perpetrators to seek damages. Consulting with an attorney is essential to explore these options.

10. Online Safety Education

Prevention is the best defense against cyber threats. Individuals can educate themselves about online safety and security through resources provided by organizations like the Electronic Frontier Foundation, the Cyberbullying Research Center, and government agencies' websites. Knowledge about potential risks and protective measures can help individuals stay safer online.

Conclusion

Facing blackmail and cyber threats is a distressing experience, but individuals should not have to endure it alone. Seeking help and support is essential for both emotional well-being and practical solutions to combat these threats. Legal assistance, reporting to authorities, cybersecurity measures, and emotional support through counseling and support groups are just a few of the resources available. It is crucial to remember that there is help and support available, and victims should not hesitate to reach out to these resources to protect themselves and take action against those who seek to harm them online. By being proactive and seeking assistance, individuals can regain control of their lives and safeguard themselves from the devastating effects of blackmail and cyber threats.

"Safeguarding from Blackmail and Online Threats" offers a comprehensive guide to protecting yourself in today's digital age. This essential resource is divided into informative chapters that address every aspect of safeguarding against blackmail and online threats. From understanding the insidious nature of blackmail and its legal implications to recognizing red flags and reporting threats, this book equips readers with the knowledge and tools needed to stay secure. With expert advice on personal safety measures, online privacy, and social media and email security, you'll learn how to fortify your digital presence.

Additionally, the book delves into cybersecurity fundamentals and provides practical insights into password management, two-factor authentication, and protecting personal documents. It also covers the crucial topic of avoiding sextortion and managing your digital footprint. For those who need assistance, the book concludes with a valuable section on seeking help and support. "Safeguarding from Blackmail and Online Threats" is your indispensable guide to maintaining your online safety and peace of mind.

ABOUT THE AUTHOR

Mr. C. P. Kumar is a retired Scientist 'G' from National Institute of Hydrology, Roorkee, Uttarakhand, India. He is also a Reiki Healer and Chakra Balancing practitioner (with pendulum dowsing) and offers Emotional Freedom Technique (EFT) to help individuals with emotional issues. Mr. Kumar has authored many books on technical, spiritual, and social topics.

For further details, you may visit his webpage
https://www.angelfire.com/nh/cpkumar/virgo.html